The Exceptional Quality of Life

Fundamentals to Start Your Life on the Right Foot

SVITLANA POWER

BALBOA
PRESS
A DIVISION OF HAY HOUSE

Copyright © 2018 Svitlana Power.

All rights reserved. No part of this book may be used or reproduced by any means, graphic, electronic, or mechanical, including photocopying, recording, taping or by any information storage retrieval system without the written permission of the author except in the case of brief quotations embodied in critical articles and reviews.

Balboa Press books may be ordered through booksellers or by contacting:

Balboa Press
A Division of Hay House
1663 Liberty Drive
Bloomington, IN 47403
www.balboapress.com
1 (877) 407-4847

Because of the dynamic nature of the Internet, any web addresses or links contained in this book may have changed since publication and may no longer be valid. The views expressed in this work are solely those of the author and do not necessarily reflect the views of the publisher, and the publisher hereby disclaims any responsibility for them.

The author of this book does not dispense medical advice or prescribe the use of any technique as a form of treatment for physical, emotional, or medical problems without the advice of a physician, either directly or indirectly. The intent of the author is only to offer information of a general nature to help you in your quest for emotional and spiritual well-being. In the event you use any of the information in this book for yourself, which is your constitutional right, the author and the publisher assume no responsibility for your actions.

Any people depicted in stock imagery provided by Getty Images are models, and such images are being used for illustrative purposes only.
Certain stock imagery © Getty Images.

Print information available on the last page.

ISBN: 978-1-9822-1608-5 (sc)
ISBN: 978-1-9822-1606-1 (hc)
ISBN: 978-1-9822-1607-8 (e)

Library of Congress Control Number: 2018913418

Balboa Press rev. date: 11/21/2018

I dedicate this book to my mom, who always loved books and had respect for any knowledge. I appreciate all the help and support from my husband, David… Thank you for the joy of togetherness, in love. Without you, this book would not be possible. To my daughter, Dar'ya, who is my best friend, and has a very special place in my heart. Thank you, my dear, for the greatest effort in supporting me in times of writing this book. To all my teachers, thank you for the support and inspiration you have given. Finally, to all the people who will apply the knowledge to create the exceptional experiences in their lives and bring the best out of yourself.

Contents

Chapter 1
The Exceptional Quality of Life is in The Details   1

Chapter 2
The Power of Clarity   7

Chapter 3
Self-Awareness Is Your "Right Hand"   21

Chapter 4
Beliefs That Support You   31

Chapter 5
The Power of a Peaceful Mind   43

Chapter 6
Create Energy for Your Life   49

Chapter 7
Finding Specific Knowledge   59

Chapter 8
The Power of the Right Order   63

Chapter 9
Discipline and Habits Should Serve You   67

Chapter 10
The Power of Focus   71

Chapter 11
Rhythm and Regularity   77

Chapter 12
Declare Ownership of Your Life   87

INTRODUCTION

Who am I, and why did I write this book? I always wanted to learn why we do what we do and what helps us to build what we want to see as a part of our life.

When I grew up, my mom was very special to me. I was loved, healthy, and happy. I loved her, and she was the model of a person I wanted to be. She was kind, and I never saw her angry or complaining about life. From memories of my childhood, I remember she wanted us to be educated and to see the world (at least on the map). At home, we had a gigantic world map on the wall. Whenever we talked about a country, Mom and all three kids looked up where it was. When we talk about the United States, I thought, without any regrets, I would never see this place, just because it is too far.

I went through many changes in my life, and so did my country, Ukraine. With significant changes in our country and us getting freedom, tough times came too. Everything that was working before did not work anymore. My education had no value just because there was no place to work. I moved to the big city and tried something different. After a few years of this journey, when I was tired from the battles of surviving in a big city, having at this moment four jobs, someone asked me, "Do you ever dream? What is your dream?" At this point, I thought, *I do not dream; I survive and barely pay bills.*

When I came home, for some reason, this question did not leave my mind; I paused for a moment and asked myself again, "What is my dream?" My timid inner voice replied, *To see the rainbow*, and I smiled. I remember the feelings of happiness I had once I saw the rainbow.

I had a picture of a waterfall with a rainbow; the power and beauty of nature impressed me so much. I would like to see the biggest and prettiest waterfall. I had never seen it in real life. One time again, I thought maybe I never would see this in real life, so I enjoyed looking at this picture. Sometimes after a long day, you look at this picture, and it makes you smile. When I melt into this image, I feel happy and delightful.

Time passed by, and my life had a new turn: I met my husband. He was born in a country with lots of waterfalls, which I did not realize yet; I didn't pay attention to it. My husband, because he knew my passion, drove long hours to show me the beautiful waterfall; we went many times on weekends to see different waterfalls. Every time, I thought

I knew the waterfalls now, but whenever I saw a new one, it surprised me more. I was so happy to be there. My best vacations were planned around big waterfalls. I went to see many of them.

We were living near a lake, and I saw a rainbow and a double rainbow many times; I saw a rainbow on top of clouds when it was raining on the ground. I asked for a rainbow and saw more: a double rainbow, the Northern lights, the moon and sun at the same time. I started to pay more attention to things I wanted to see.

"The quality of your life is the quality of where you live emotionally" (Tony Robbins). At that moment, I was on cloud nine. After this phenomenal transformation in my life, I had a dream to help others realize their dreams.

Another story that affected my life: A few years ago, I organized a woman's club. In my 2015 New Year resolution, I wrote: "I want to organize a club for women to inspire and support them, and use the power of community to have a strong foundation in our lives." Later, I came across my earlier resolutions from 2013 and 2014 in which I wrote the same sentence about my dream club. After this, I told my friend at work about it. This day, she organized five people for this club. That's how my dream began to unfold. I learned then that if I wrote down my dreams more frequently, I would remember what is vital for me, and if I reach out to others about my dreams, someone could help me sooner.

Chapter 1

The Exceptional Quality of Life is in The Details

Details create the big picture.
—Sanford I. Weill

First, how do we define a quality of life?

Let's draw two pictures: 😊 ☹ With a small difference in details.

By paying attention to details of your life, you will make the difference you need to be happy. You are the creator of your experiences.

The small details on these pictures tell us a lot about the person we see. With those details, the whole story changes. It doesn't matter how big a project is, whether it is your education or just your meal for today, you need to pay attention to create quality.

Let's imagine two similar shirts. One of them is of excellent quality, and the other is not. At first glance, they look the same and serve the same purpose. When you start to focus on small details, you notice the differences. What kind of material? What kind of stitches? How straight are the stitches and how strong? How long will this shirt last? How many decorative details does it have? All these things affect the aesthetic look and overall quality of the shirt.

You can make a difference in your daily cup of coffee. Drinking coffee in a peaceful backyard will be much more pleasurable than a rushed cup of coffee in the car.

Pay attention to the small things. Quality is the big picture. To build it, find small pieces of it first. Start with the parts of it, and you can then put together the big picture. Pull the threads of connection to the excellent life you desire. Make excellence comfortable and familiar to you, and your life will be changed because it will become second nature.

Commit today to pursuing an excellent life: be your best, do your best, give your best, expect the best, and accept nothing but the best.

Quality is made by people who were inspired and who knew their job and did it well.

What does it look like in detail?

- quality meals
- quality work
- quality time with yourself
- quality time with somebody
- quality relationships
- quality minutes, hours, days

There is the teaching: "To grow, you need to step out of your comfort zone." Pay attention to details; you need to expand your comfort zone, not leave one and get another. Always expand; remove the barriers to make your comfort zone bigger and feel more grounded in the zone you already have.

Three Things to Remember

1. Know how quality looks and feels.
2. Know where to find an example of the quality you want.
3. Make connections with things you want to have and things you want to do, and find the people you like among those you need to know.

Chapter 2

The Power of Clarity

"Which road do I take?"
"Where do you want to go?"
"I don't much care."
"Then it doesn't matter which way you go."
—Lewis Carroll, *Alice's Adventures in Wonderland*

Imagine if everything is possible, and you can be, do, and have anything you want. Describe in detail how your excellent life looks.

Your answer _____

Spend some time to understand what your extraordinary life is like. Go to your dream vision. When we're kids, everything is possible for us, isn't it?

Where did you see an example of your dream?

Your answer _____

What is your ideal health?

Your answer _____

What are the small details of it?

Your answer _____

Do you have it now? When did you have it?

Your answer _____

How does your ideal relationship look?

Your answer _____

If you feel sad, why must it be that way forever?

Your answer _____

When did you come up with this conclusion?

Your answer _____

Many of us will say, "I don't know," and never think about it again. Keep asking yourself until you find out the answer. You need to know it.

Do you believe there is a way for you to achieve your ideal weight? Did you think that there isn't? The reality is, millions of people never have a problem with their weight. What do these people think about food overall? What do they think when they are eating? What are their routines for meal preparation? What do they think about themselves?

You need to notice what they do differently than you. There are no details too small; you need to be curious about everything. You do not need to talk. Look around and maybe go to dinner with someone who has no problem with weight. Notice the differences. Do not assume you know it all. Be patient, and watch everything. Notice how long it takes the person to cook, what their feelings area about the meal, and their table manners. Now you need to use your imagination. What if it's possible for you to never have a problem with your weight? The first time you think about it, your brain will go crazy. Don't mind it. Continue smiling and imagine again.

Now, ask yourself, "If it's normal and healthy for other people to have it, why am I accepting less?"

Your answer _____

Does it absolutely have to be the way it is now?

Your answer _____

How can you change it for the better? How can you make this easy, almost automatic?

Your answer _____

If there is the way for you to have it, how can you do it?

Your answer _____

I recommend doing the same work in different areas of your life.

Which relationship is ideal for you?

Your answer _____

What kind of daily routine can serve it?

Your answer _____

What can you do every day to lead you where you want to reach?

Your answer _____

For example, get up earlier, take a minute to pray or meditate or set expectations to have fun today, drink water, exercise, and have breakfast. Maybe there is one thing you can do consistently, like eat at the same time and the same amount of food. For example, eat your dinner at six o'clock, and you won't want to eat at eight or nine. There are many variants, so you need to experiment and find which ones can work for you.

Who do you need to become to be happy?

Your answer _____

What income would you like to have? What amount can make you happy? How much? How often?

Your answer _____

What are your ideal places to live and work? What do they feel and look like?

Your answer _____

The Exceptional Quality of Life 13

What kind of habits may help?

Your answer _____

What is making you happy?

Your answer _____

Knowing the answers will help you to evaluate and do more of what adds value to your life and less of what does not.

The clarity of your vision, desires, and expectations helps you to focus on what is more important now.

We all think in pictures. When you find what speaks to you, it brings responses in your body.

When you are thirsty, that is when you will be at the peak of foretaste of having a drink. Your body responds stronger before you drink. After you drink half a glass, the water does not have the same response in your body. As life shows, it feels stronger before you have it. As it becomes normal for you to have it, your feelings have less control over time. And as you eat, the first bites are the best. After your appetite is satisfied, your feelings fade, and a new desire will be born.

It's important to understand the difference between feeling lack of water and the foretaste of drinking the water. You need to feel, "Wow," before it happens in real life. Feel the feelings that occur in your mind of your ideal future. Enjoy that moment now. Your physiology must respond with feelings before things start coming true.

For example, in Pavlov's experiments with dogs, he taught the dog to salivate at the sound of a bell, without the food. The dog responded with attention and excitement, evidenced by sniffing around and drooling. His physiology changed because he expected to have some food.

It is important to know what you want in life, not what you can afford at this moment or can do from where you are now. You need to have a vision of good things in your life. Take your time to dream and plan before you even try to understand how you will achieve this.

If you struggle to have a clear vision of how your prosperous future may look, imagine everything is possible. If you don't expect anything good anymore and think it is your destiny to struggle because you are not normal or lucky, I suggest you start by questioning this belief. When did you adopt it? Who made you believe in it? Did things change over time? Have you grown up? Do you have more experience now?

You are who you are. You are in the place you are, and from there, you can go anywhere you choose. Imagine yourself at the end of your life. What do you want to experience before your last moment? What do you want to say to your friends? What kind of advice would you give to yourself? What do you want people to say about you after you are gone? Who do you want to be with you at the moment you die? What kind of relationships do you want to experience?

Consider this: We are all equal on the earth—rich and poor, healthy and not, smart and not, talented and not, lucky and unlucky. Do you think these are just words? People play different roles in life: baby, kid, adult, spouse or partner, employee or manager, and many more. Do you agree? Imagine yourself an actor in a movie. What kind of role are you playing? Can you get another role? Maybe next season, you choose to play the main character. Unless you pick up the initiative and decide you want the leading role, it is never going to happen. You need to try many things for one to work out well. Set new priorities. Notice which actions are from a different movie.

Look closely at yourself, your habits, your reaction. Journal your good days and glorious moments. Notice who was with you and what you did today to feel this. Start watching your thoughts and feelings, and learn how your body reacts to different people and situations. The secret is, not everything will improve and change at the same time. Changes require some time. The habits and character traits from your last movie may not be helpful in your new vision for life.

Do you analyze and multitask to the point you feel overwhelmed? Do you feel like a new driver on a five-lane highway? When I was learning to drive, I was overwhelmed and terrified.

I told my friend my concerns: "I don't even know where to look on the highway."

She replied with a simple answer, which helped me a lot: "You are responsible not to hit the car in front of you. Your main concern is to keep a safe distance from the car ahead of you, so in case of an emergency, you have the time to react."

It is similar when you work on yourself. Change one habit at a time; complete one challenge at a time.

Keep in mind there are many ways to get to a place where you want to be, and you should use more than one method. If one doesn't work, you have many more to experiment with, to get the result you desire. One method is fast; five methods are five times faster.

For example, if you want to learn English, you can go to college or take an ESL course, watch Youtube tutorials, watch English movies, and read English books. The key is having commitment to success and being flexible on the way to get there. It means, I do not know how, but I am going to do it. I am sure something will bring me the result I expect, and I will be at peace with myself, and the challenge will be complete.

For example, think about a shopping list.

It's easy for you to shop when you know what you need before you go to the store. It even determines which store you go to. Does it make any sense to go to the grocery store if you are about to buy a car? You might say, "I would love to buy a car, but all I can afford is groceries." I am telling you to be clear about what you want to have, not what you can have at this moment. Get clarity about your image, your style of life, your education, and so on.

When you are clear about the image for yourself to live the life you want, you will rehearse the role you want to play mentally, and you will practice it physically. With time and some effort, you will master the game to perfection. You will find out all possible information about what education you need, the people you need to know, and the image of yourself you need to develop. You will put the pieces together to move in the direction you need to go. You know what you need: how it looks, how it feels, how it sounds, and even how it smells.

Use hearing, sight, and touch to remind you what you want. I see pictures, examples in real life. I feel good, easy, and delightful. I know the sound of it: for some, it's a river sound; for others, it's the noise of a big city. For you, it may be the sound of new shoes or a baby laughing. I collect information and facts supporting the idea. I create the belief I need by repeating thoughts and emotions supporting the idea.

Create a new image of yourself, a new story. You know what you want. Who knows how to get there? Make connections with your future: blend in, tune in, and join the people who are two steps ahead of you.

When you are clear about the place you want to live, you will find a way to make it as close to your ideal as possible. You will clean up, you will renovate, you will sell or buy, and it will be your pleasure to work on it.

Clarity is not saying, "Go somewhere, I do not know where, and bring me something, which I do not know what." Things you need will be much easier to find with open eyes, than by touch under a blanket, especially if you have no idea what you need to find.

Get clarity about experiences you would love to have. For example, you know for sure that you don't want to have any kids. When a guy speaks to you about having a big family, you need to be able to explain your position about kids. That is not easy, because at this moment, you may be afraid and question yourself.

Look at the big picture: imagine you push yourself, and you have three kids and never overcome your feelings. Because you are not happy, the guy can't explain why things happen the way they happen, and you both want a divorce. It's so far back, and now it's piled up with dirty socks or many more reasons.

You will not be living life afraid to lose the guy because he never was on the same page. You know what you want and what you don't. You will not be stuck with nonsense; this is the only chance to have a partner. It is an example, and it's possible the guy will want to be with you anyway. With time, it's possible you can change your mind, but the conversation must happen, and you need to let your partner know your vision for the life you want.

Get clarity about how much money you want to have. When you are clear about how much money you want to have, you will never accept something that cannot bring you the amount you desire (unless it is one step on the path to your dream).

The vocabulary of a successful person includes a vision for your future, positive mind-set, imagination, and expectation.

Three Things to Remember

1. It's always better to be neat, clean, and organized because it works. Organize your enviroment to make it convenient, pleasurable, and meaningful for you.
2. It's easier to organize your thoughts, ideas, and beliefs, when you bring everything out in front of you on paper, so you can see it and arrange it.
3. It's time to renew or fix anything old or broken, or else let it go. Even if it's an old idea, reevaluate and decide to either act on it now or let it go and give the space for a new idea.

CHAPTER 3

Self-Awareness Is Your "Right Hand"

Self-awareness opens the door to better decision making and a fulfilling, happy life. Emotional changes are more difficult to develop than physical, but physical changes can affect your emotions. When you're in control of material things around you, your emotional state will normalize too; it works the opposite way, as well. When you are in control of the direction you are going and the emotions you are carrying, your physical world will change. The better you feel, the stronger will be the impulse to create necessary changes.

Peace, Balance, and Stability

Your actions are mindful when you are in harmony and peace. You are organized, peaceful, and happy if you want to be. At the end of the day, the person who *wants to succeed* will succeed.

To be aware of what happens to you, what makes you feel the way you feel is the foundation of a happy life. When you start to watch yourself, you begin to notice:

- Some thoughts make you smile; some make you feel blue.
- Some beliefs make you act bold, and some stop you before you make the first move.

- Some actions make you feel good; some make you feel tired and exhausted without any result or benefits.
- Some people make you feel good about life, yourself, and the things you do; some make you feel miserable.

To get peace, you need to want it; you need to search for it. You need to recognize stress and avoid it when you can. We think irritation and stress are about big things; they can be a complex of small things too. How well you rest the night before will affect how you react to everything the next day. You can have these habits: wanting to prove I am right and you are wrong, overeating, oversleeping, not sleeping enough, and so on. You do it over and over, not paying attention; it affects you the next day. It is small, but a million little things can become a huge problem. You cannot explain a week later why you started to cry after a button fell off your jacket.

Manage your stress. Manage how you see the situation; mindfully imagine the case in a different time, in a different place, or with different people. It may look stupid or funny. Do you take your fair share of responsibility? Do you take control of the situation? Sometimes, people take responsibility for their whole family and are surprised when the people around them are not happy. They do not even realize they're showing mistrust to family members, and their expectations are wrong. Maybe it's easier and faster to do it by yourself, but it's a quick fix that will not last.

Resting and making your body stronger will help you handle any situation. What do you do to regenerate your energy? Some people take a drink, some overeat, some clean house, some work hard, some fight. Is it healthy to do so? Fix the problem the way it will not need to be fixed again tomorrow. Use your senses to help you; ask yourself how it feels. Is it pure and light energy? Is it flow? Increase your standards; create a new image of yourself. If you don't like what you are doing, ask yourself, is it necessary to be like that? Is this the best I can do?

Respect your home, take care of it, make it comfortable and pleasurable to be there. Clean the place you live and work so that it can function better and you use the space more effectively.

Love, respect, and care for yourself. Take care of your body and take control of it. Take control of your body emotionally, physically, mentally. Who is the boss, you or your emotions? Is a dog wagging its tail, or the tail wagging its dog? Do you tell your body what to do, or does your body run your life?

Clean up, lose weight, and find your style of life. Take control back; take responsibility. Take control of your surrounding environment, and be around people you want to be with. Repeat the same system in every area of your life. Clean up and take over control.

Free yourself from habits that are against your health

and well-being. There is freedom of choice on a daily basis; everything is allowed, but not everything is good for you.

This is the real holy trinity: physical health, emotional health, and mental health. Our body, soul, and mind must go in the same direction. All three are part of one and must settle to be happy together and perform well. For this, there must be better communication between them; each one has its voice and must listen to the others. Those three must always be in agreement and love unconditionally.

Be open to the possibilities. One thing leads to another. What if I could be successful? I would think like a successful person. I would believe I am good for it. I would act like a successful person, and good things would happen to me. I would know life is supporting me all the time. I would appreciate all that I have and do, and I would enjoy every small good thing of my life.

We all know people who come in the room like the sun in the morning, and other people do not want to speak to anyone. If you ask someone like that, they cannot even explain what happens to them. It can be a small thing that happens many times, and that creates a problem. If your day begins wrong, all day goes wrong. There is a saying, "What goes around comes around." Your mood contagious, and people unconsciously read your state and respond like magnets.

When you are sad, you will look for another reason to be sad; when are you deeply upset, you will find other reasons to cry. At this moment, you are not in control of your emotions; you're on autopilot. Your mind focuses on finding things to support your feelings. When you are peaceful, you take control of your emotions, and the good feelings return to you. You may say it is easy to talk; try to calm down when all your body is shaking with anger or injustice. You need to distract your focus with something else, like interrupting a crying kid with a toy.

Did you know, you can pay attention to how you are breathing, and it will make an enormous difference for you? When you upset, your breathing is different than in your normal state. Normalizing the rhythm of your breathing will help you feel better. Open a window to get some fresh air in the room, or walk outside; yoga, kung fu, or other sports can help your breathing.

Did you know, you have the power to police your thoughts? You can change them. Your opinions define your expectations. When your brain is sending the signal "It is cold outside," you will dress warm, but sometimes, you speak back to yourself, saying that it's warm outside and you'll be okay, so you don't need a coat today.

Change your thoughts and reactions, and remind yourself what you want. Leave some reminders around the house, like notes and pictures of a particular place you want to go or an experience you want to have; all of this will help keep your focus and move in the direction you need to go.

You may think, *How can I forget what I want? Why do I need these reminders?* There are lots of choices every day, and it's easy to get distracted by small things. You want to be skinny, but you have a party coming up soon, and you like to cook, and you need to clean house today, and you have to go to school and speak with teacher; you also want to have money and travel the world and have lovely clothes. Did you notice how far the thought about being skinny is now? Imagine you have a child, and this all the kid wants. When you are a parent, will you give what is easier for you to distract the attention of the kid, for him to stop crying? Your mind gives you something fast to make you stop crying for a moment. The problem with this is, it's a quick fix; it's not permanent.

The good news is, you can have it all, just by planning and enjoying the process of implementation. By doing this, you are allowing your significant wants come first; the little wishes need to give way to the seniors.

For a while, put emotions aside and compare without judgments. Know what you want to have, what you want to do, and who you want to be. Ask yourself how long you've had this problem. How long do you think you need to fix it? It's possible you will realize this problem's been with you for twenty years, and it's about time to fix it.

Three Things to Remember

1. Traveling helps you to see things from a different perspective. You don't need to go far, just a different area than you are used to going.
2. Traveling will affect your emotional state. It also helps you to be less attached to places and things.
3. Interaction with new people will give you fresh ideas and examples of what you may like to do, who you want to become, or what you wish to have.

Chapter 4

Beliefs That Support You

Repeating your thoughts creates beliefs. Repeated thoughts supported by emotions become great beliefs; with time, these beliefs stop serving you and become a significant resistance to your wishes in life.

Nothing stays the same; things look different in a different place with different people. With time, people change their beliefs; it's a part of the evolution process. The people around you, the thoughts you have, the feelings you experience create your beliefs. Beliefs determine your expectations; expectations set your behavior.

You can believe in whatever you want. I'm not talking about religion; it's about thoughts you have every day. For example, "Success comes with hard work." Is it possible this is not the same for everyone? What if making money and having abundance in your life came naturally? What if you were born in a successful family? I am not promoting a lazy style of life, just supporting my point. There is more than one way to get an abundant life; creativity is helpful.

You start to support any thoughts with facts, examples, and emotions. Where did you see it? When you enjoy doing something, it's not hard work anymore. Saying it's hard makes it harder, and if you don't like what you do, you can change it.

Maybe at this moment, your beliefs are true for you, but they are not serving you well. Some of your thoughts don't help you by any means; by default, they are running on the back of your mind. You keep them and enjoy the process of torturing yourself.

You may ask, "Is it possible that people can enjoy pain?" Yes, if in your mind, they are so wrong, you are the victim, or you were told to be proud of yourself, you need to go through lots of pain because life isn't fair. You can't help but start to become used to pain and even enjoy the process. It's like an itch; the more you scratch, the more it itches, and you want to scratch it more, even if you know it's not good for you.

You can do anything and think anything, but not everything is right for you. If you are a friend to yourself, you will carefully choose your thoughts and actions; think twice about old conclusions that became your beliefs.

Observe a ballet performance: It looks so easy and effortless. The reality is, every movement is under control, and it's not as easy for the dancers as it looks. It's clear: the ballerinas are passionate about their dance, and they spend lots of time practicing their moves.

You may say, "I would love to have a good family, but I don't." Is it a problem, or is it a pattern of thoughts affecting your behavior?

It's possible to think you want to have a family, but you cannot allow yourself to have it because you believe there's lots of work involved. It may be true, and yet, you contradict yourself, and you stay where you started, never moving ahead.

By thinking over and over about the great amount of work, the fear is blown out of proportion. What if you start to question it and ask yourself if it is indeed so frightening?

Your thoughts, emotions, and actions must be going in same dirrection:

- ✓ Thoughts: intention to succeed
- ✓ Special mood: relaxation, peace, joy, and excitement
- ✓ Actions: based on the subconscious program; make sure it's a good program

You may say, "I would love to learn something, but my memory is terrible." Is it a problem, or is it a pattern of thoughts affecting your behavior?

By saying, "My memory is terrible," you are not giving yourself a chance to experiment. It's like, "Cut the head off now." You do not put any effort to remember because you are saying that your memory is bad, period. There is no room in your mind for improvement or any effort to remember. With time, your memory becomes worse because you are not exercising to improve it. You maybe think, *That's not true: I tried many times, but it did not work.* Now try this: You need to memorize a phone number, period; this is the number in the case of emergency. You need to know this number. Will you remember it?

- ✓ Thoughts: intention to succeed
- ✓ Special mood: relaxation, peace, joy, and excitement
- ✓ Actions: based on the subconscious program; make sure it's a good program

You may say, "I would love to be happy, but it won't happen to me." Is it a problem, or is it a pattern of thoughts affecting your behavior?

"My life is not going well, and there is nothing good to expect in the future. How can I be happy?" That might be your truth at the moment, but thinking these thoughts over and over does not help a bit. Do your best and leave God the rest, but hear me out: do your best. You think you can't because you are not in the mood? In this case, you need to relax and be happy just for a moment; be cheerful where you are now.

How do you do that? You can buy ice cream or drink a cup of coffee if that's what makes you feel better; you can go to the park and feed the birds, or watch a comedy, or speak with your friend. These things may not be what you like to do; everyone is different. Do what you enjoy, and it won't do you any harm. Being happy temporarily will not change your life, but it will improve your mood and make your day better. One good day gives you time to figure your next step toward your dream life.

- ✓ Thoughts: intention to succeed
- ✓ Special approach: relaxation, peace, joy, and excitement
- ✓ Actions: based on the subconscious program; make sure it's a good program

You may say, "I wish to be married, but I always find trouble instead of joy in relationships." Is it a problem, or is it a pattern of behavior?

You want to date someone, but it's not something you usually do. Observe yourself for some time. What comes to mind? Is it, "I feel good about myself, and I am happy to go for a date," or is it, "Why would he love me? I am not beautiful or smart or wealthy. There is no such thing as love. You're in love and happy until you get married; marriage ruins a good relationship." That may feel true for you at this moment, but negative thoughts won't help you succeed in building an easy and fun relationship.

Imagine you keep thinking, *I am not beautiful*, and you go on a date. Will you be able to enjoy your evening? Even if the evening goes well, there will always be fear: "Now it's good, but he won't want to see me again."

It would help if you relaxed and put in the effort to enjoy a date. You enjoy yourself as you prepare for the date; you decide what would be fun to do, to eat, to drink, to talk about. If today was your last date, have one wonderful evening to remember. Maybe you didn't even kiss each other but only had a good conversation at dinner; not every date finishes with marriage, but life is more peaceful and fun when good things happen. During the first date, don't put lots of hope for the future; enjoy yourself and show small signs that you want to go out again. This way everything will go well.

You'll notice this date is more comfortable for both of you. Your partner will feel this easiness and want to be with you again. Your joy makes him content too. When it's easy and fun you want to do it again, don't you? For this to happen, you need to support yourself with one more thought: *I will have a good relationship, with this person or somebody else. I will build the relationship I want to have.* Why? You are awesome. That's the reason. Put a smile on your face; be more playful. Try it out.

- ✓ Thoughts: intention to succeed
- ✓ Special mood: relaxation, peace, joy, and excitement
- ✓ Actions: based on the subconscious program; make sure it's a good program

You may say, "I want to have more money, but there is no way for me to become wealthy." Is it a problem, or is it a pattern of thoughts affecting your behavior?

There are many reasons why this is not a problem. Let's say there is a way for you to become wealthy, but you don't know how. What you need is the intention to look for the way.

Let's imagine you put away one hundred dollars to start to build your capital, and next month, you add fifty dollars to have some spending money. That's not a lot of money; it's just a game: "I have it." You go out of the store, and you still have money. Do you feel good about it? Do you feel better about yourself? You will say, "A hundred bucks is not the money I want to have." The truth is, once you learn to manage $100, you'll be able to manage $1,000 and $10,000 the same way as you did with $100.

Later, you want to put aside a little bit more, and you start to enjoy the process of having money and managing it; at the end of the month, you have more. Next, you'll notice you find a way to earn a little bit more and put away more, and you skip buying unnecessary stuff. You see this is going easier.

First, you play and see what happens. Later, you master the game; you learn some rules, improve your technique, and play to win. Do you think you have a chance now? At the end of the day, the one who wanted to succeed will succeed.

- ✓ Thoughts: intention to succeed
- ✓ The special frame of mind: relaxation, peace, joy, and excitement
- ✓ Actions: based on the subconscious program; make sure it's a good program

Self-Esteem

There is a saying: A spoon of tar spoils a barrel of honey.

Does the level of self-confidence affect how much money you make? I am learning to invest in myself and getting better because my future depends on it.

> Self-esteem: the ability to look at
> yourself as having the value.
> —Dr. John Nemian

Strong self-confidence and a clear vision of your future are what it takes to be successful in life. What if you don't see anything good coming your way in the future? You keep looking for what you'd like to have and do. Ask yourself if you could see yourself having it, what would you do to get it? Do not accept the first quick answer, as taking it from someone will not bring you anything but trouble. There is a way without any harm to yourself or others; keep asking. Your intentions must be a joy for you and benefit the people around you. Your inner self will find it for you, as long as you stay on the subject long enough. When you recognize, with every fiber of your being, that you deserve to earn more for no other reason than you are worth it, you will.

- ✓ Always have some money. Be aware of Parkinson's law: expenditures rise to meet income.
- ✓ The law of attraction says that you attract into your life those things that are in harmony with your dominant thoughts. Thoughts are causes, and conditions are an effect. Therefore, the quality of your thinking largely determines the quality of your life.
- ✓ How much value you represent controls how much money you will have. Focus on service for a million people, and start with one person.

Three Things to Remember

1. Be open to possibilities. What if life can be comfortable? What if you don't always need to struggle?
2. It will not hurt if you play the role of a happy, blessed, and wealthy person. Even if it's not exactly true at this moment, you'll practice feeling happy and lucky.
3. When you do all these things, you may not receive what you're expecting instantaneously; regardless, do not create drama. Don't give up hope; something even better will come along eventually.

Chapter 5

The Power of a Peaceful Mind

I was curious about what was common to happiness, health, and wealth? It's laughter, acting with enthusiasm, light energy, and a peaceful mind. What's an essential quality of the past, present, and future? It is the quality of now. If today is good, tomorrow, you will have had a good yesterday, and you'll have momentum going forward to the day after.

Wherever you are, be there. Smell the roses. It's very important to have peace of mind, to know what to do, and to have the power to do so; being in a relaxed and peaceful state is half the deal. Drawing pictures, sewing something, washing dishes, cleaning the house, or organizing things gives you a sense of accomplishment and makes you feel like you have things under control.

Once you are in the correct mind-set, you can begin to figure out which way to turn to get to your desired destination. You can use images to visualize this more clearly and help you build plans for your future.

Take control of your mind. Calm your mind with prayers, meditations, affirmations, walks, drawing, sewing, playing with your kids, doing something pleasurable for yourself. Build plans for your wants, find pictures that speak to you, and enjoy the process. Your inner self knows how to get where you want to be; everything is possible for you.

Forgiveness, gratitude, trust, and love will bring you peace, balance, and stability. Let go of heavy feelings, and let God take care of it.

Praying: A conversation with God, or a solemn request for help or expression of thanks, addressed to God. You can do it anytime, anywhere, and for as long as you want.

Meditation: Relaxing your mind to regain your energy. The recommended amount of time spent meditating is twenty-four minutes, as we have twenty-four hours every day.

Mantra: A calming word, thought, or phrase repeated silently; this is very useful in preventing distracting thoughts.

Yoga: Healthy posture plus mindful meditations.

Doing yoga, you breathe in and out, and your body is in slow motion. You can't change direction if you are on high speed. You need to slow down when you don't know where you need to go, or even come to a complete stop.

Three Things to Remember

1. Nothing good will be born if you are not in the proper mood and peaceful state of mind.
2. When you notice your emotions are not stable, take a break, interrupt your thoughts, occupy your mind. It can take some time, but it's worth it.
3. Everything that you did before this moment creates your experience now. Let's say you are not in a good

mood, and somebody tells you a compliment. It won't be the same as if you felt amazing before they told you the compliment. When you are in a good mood, you react differently.

Chapter 6

Create Energy for Your Life

What is energy?

Definition: the strength and vitality required for sustained physical or mental activity.

My understanding: It is power, life, momentum, and revolution; these are all things we use to describe energy. Have you ever heard someone say, "This place needs some energy," or "This person needs some energy," or "This is lifeless"? That means this place or person needs to make some changes, to get more life.

What do we know about the energy we want and need to feel strong? The most powerful energy is supported by emotions. Emotional energy is unstoppable. When you are curious and sincerely wish for something, when you are in love, or when you're creating something, your feelings automatically become strong. Yes, they can be even stronger when you are mad or upset, but you know the direction it's leading you. Do you want to burn up to the point when you feel exhausted? Create energy for life by building momentum.

All emotions are powerful. Some of them work for us, and some of them destroy us. Love, passion, curiosity, excitement, flying high: Those are good for you. Anger, sadness, hate: Those are powerful, but they are not part of a happy and successful life. If you stick with them for a while, you'll find yourself going nowhere.

You don't need to accept everything that life has to offer; you can choose to take what is a part of a good life and drop everything else.

You may think, *How can I drop it, if someone is annoying me all the time?* Think again; the event happens once, or you contact this person for some time and later replay the situation in your mind many more times. How long? You decide, but first you need to notice it. Sometimes, when your emotions are very strong at the moment things happen, you keep it in your mind for years; some people keep the story in mind for life, telling what happens with the same support of strong emotions to next generation.

Even if you don't speak about it, people around still read your emotions, and your actions will be in tune with those emotions. They are destroying you; that's why you need to find a way to release emotions like that. There are ways to do it properly.

Emotions can be light and bright or heavy and dark; they can touch you deeply. Avoid the drama.

To have the energy, you need to have a continual source of power and be careful where you spend it. What does it mean? Many desperate people look exhausted because so many emotions are going nowhere or bad habits are destroying all they built.

Imagine a wild young horse; for you to use his power, and for the horse to serve you, you need to make him obey, to break him in. You want to pay attention to where you direct your energy. Is it serving you or acting like a horse? You are the human; you can choose your reaction and control your emotions.

Conclusion: Energy must be spent in the right direction. Taking control of your emotions and going in the direction you need will make your life much more stable and peaceful.

Enjoy the movement where you set up yourself for success. Attach yourself to a big train, which goes in the direction you want to go. If you know some class, some course, some person, some style of life that will automatically bring you the life you want, join it. Next, watch what happens: on this journey, there will be many like-minded people coming into your life, and this alone will make you stronger.

Energy flows where attention goes. Pay attention to the good things and improvements. Help yourself to remember with elastic on your wrist, a card in your pocket, a picture, or some other reminder. Add some love and passion to this, and your power will multiply.

A sample affirmation: "I can! I am in control. I love myself. My reward is on my way. The result I want and have been working on is very close."

Believe in your new reality. You don't believe in affirmations? They work like commercials and ads. There are advertisements everywhere you go. You eat, and they're there; you go to bed, and they're there with you again. Does advertising work? It may not work the first time you see it, but after you see it the third or fifth time, it will work when it's relevant to your situation. It's the same with your new reality: when you start to think about it as a part of your life, you'll look for your way to get it.

Sometimes, you feel like you don't have any energy. That's when you need some rest, evaluation, and adjusting some actions and direction you are going. Maybe you need to improve your health or change your sleeping or eating habits.

If you look closer at what exactly makes you feel strong or weak, it's relationships with yourself, loved ones, and friends.

Imagine you invested in something and lost your money, and now you are upset. When you follow your thoughts, you will notice, if you had doubts in yourself before, you now say to yourself, "I am stupid," or "I did it again, and Bill told me I never get anything right."

But if you're strong inside, you say to yourself, "Yes, I made a mistake, and now I need to fix it."

That's all; there is no drama for years. If your family members make jokes about your investments, and you weren't strong before, you beat yourself up. This way, you never have power, real power, when you accumulate power within you. When you support yourself and have your emotions under your control, you have power. You feel strong and healthy.

How can you save energy?

You can stop participating in negative emotions. Walk away

from fighting and arguments. Say you need to go somewhere right now, or you'll talk about it later. If this fighting is in your mind, notice it and say to yourself, "That's enough; stop it." Interrupt your thoughts with some business or talk to some other person or pray or meditate or take a nap. Repeat affirmations and words of support to yourself. You can't be against yourself; you want to fix the problem, improve a situation, and build up your self-confidence.

There are two ways to be strong: to be an oak or a willow tree. In a time of natural disaster, like a storm or strong wind, you need to be flexible to make the power of wind softer. Like a willow tree, you become softer and allow the wind to blow past your branches. This way, the wind can't break them. You need to save your energy and walk away from a fight. What is most important, to be right or to be happy? When you take your emotions under control, you can explain yourself well without hurting anyone. It doesn't mean you are hiding from your problems; it means you do not fight against what you have no power to change.

Keep in your mind that after every storm, there will be a calm morning. When the storm passes by, you become as strong as an oak. You know what you want and where you are going. You stay straight and powerful.

You are a machine that generates energy, and you are the one to use this power. You're in control of when you spend your energy and where. The classic way to create a good drive is to do good to others, to feel good about yourself. Educate yourself to make your life more interesting, more fulfilling.

Energy moves automobiles, grows plants, warms our hands, and helps us to move around. When you move around, you generate energy. Ask yourself, how can you create more of it? Is it going to a gym? Is it going for a walk with your dog? Is it jumping on a trampoline? Is it dancing? Is it swimming? Is it making love with the person you love?

You need to have energy to live life to the fullest and time to speed up your experience. You need to want to do what you need to do. When you know you need to do it, and it's not your favorite thing, you can attach to that something that you do like, and it will be more comfortable for you. Also, reward yourself with pleasure; create little celebration after you complete your task.

How do you attach what you love to do to what needs to be done, in a stress-free and fun way? Let's say I like listening to music or watching a movie; nowadays, technology allows us to exercise, watch a movie, or listen to an audiobook. Now you are no longer counting how many days you went to the gym; you're counting seasons of a show you've watched. It becomes easy to exercise, and you enjoy doing so.

There is a shift from difficult to simple. Now, your energy flows with ease. There is no resistance; there is no focus on the weight you need to lose or spending long hours exercising. You enjoy your healthy body, and it starts to serve you better automatically. You may say, "I never liked to do exercises," but did you try dancing, jumping, or skiing? Any movement is good. Consistent daily actions will create habits. Habits create compounding results over time.

Passion and Fulfillment

The best motivation is curiosity. Interest makes doing things easy and fun. What is touching your heart? What makes you smile when you talk about it? What makes you feel good? Try something and stick with it for a while. Know more than others about it, spend more time on it, be the best at it. You don't need to be strict and stubborn; be flexible and open to new ideas coming from the initial engagement.

Spend some time watching yourself; remind yourself what kind of games you played as a child. Do you like to sit on the sofa with a blanket and read? Continue to do it, and who knows, maybe you will start to write a book or you'll invent a more comfortable couch.

The contrast shows you what you want and what you don't want. You have the impulse to change the situation, and you are looking for support for things to change.

Healthy eating will affect your energy level big time. Maybe you were never interested in nutrition and have no idea what kind of food makes you feel better. Yes, you need to spend some time learning about it, but then you can apply that knowledge in real life.

Actions: Neat, Fresh, and Impressive

Do it now. Be up to speed with your wishes, listen to your heart, and reply with actions.

There are many ways to get to the place you want to be; you can try many of them too. If one doesn't work, another will. One is fast; five are five times faster.

Make a commitment; say, "I don't know how, but I'm going to do it, and if it's not with this person, it'll be with somebody else."

If you did everything that you can, and it didn't work, it's possible you are very close.

Think about the result. Think long term. Fix the problem so it does not need to be fixed again tomorrow. See the big picture. Check your priorities.

Three Things to Remember

1. Having a proper relationship with yourself, taking care of yourself, and making an effort to improve will give you lots of energy.
2. Having your energy under control will give you even more energy.
3. Being active, having initiative, and showing curiosity will give you energy for life.

Chapter 7

Finding Specific Knowledge

If something doesn't work, it means
you don't know something.
—Brian Tracy

Knowledge must be specific; a spoon is essential for dinner. To do your best, you need to know what to do. You learn in theory and practice. When you listen to somebody and don't understand what they're saying, they either don't speak your language or are at another level. Professors and bankers, philosophers and carpenters talk in different styles about the same stuff; if nothing is familiar to you, or you find it difficult to attach to what you already know, you'll learn nothing. It's like a train attaching new carriages; you to connect the unfamiliar to what you already know.

Health, relationships, money, and careers are all different subjects to study. Each subject has rules and actions you need to know about. When you are cooking soup, it doesn't matter how much you know about history or biology; all that matters is how much you know about cooking. If it's a good family that's important to you, you need to know how a decent family looks in your mind and feels in your heart. If in your mind you keep saying, "It's not possible with my luck," "It won't work for our family," "I don't even know what a good family is," or "I'm stressed all the time without a family," guess how soon you'll have a family?

Little by little, by paying attention to details, you start to learn; you watch for examples and begin to notice what works for you. When you feel good about yourself, you'll act more natural with a partner and the whole dating thing. You know precisely how a great family looks and feels; you'll know what people do to enjoy their date and what they don't do.

As an example of specific knowledge, say I want to learn English. Which of these is most essential for me right now?

- grammar
- speaking
- reading
- pronunciation
- vocabulary

You may think you need to know them all, but in a specific situation, what you need will be different. If you're talking with an English speaker, you need to learn vocabulary and phrases; if you're writing ESL test, you need to learn grammar.

Chapter 8

The Power of the Right Order

The Exceptional Quality of Life   65

The order you do things is critical.

Example 1: Cooking soup. There is a particular order in which you prepare soup.

1. Get a pot out.
2. Fill it with water.
3. Put it on the stove.
4. Turn on the gas.
5. Cut up the vegetables and meat, and put them into the pot.
6. Give it some time.
7. Season it.

> You cannot turn the stove on if there's no water in the pot, and you can't add water if you do not have a pot.

First, you have to know what kind of dish you are cooking. Next, you need a good recipe, the right ingredients, and time.

It's the same with relationships: You need self-respect, a clear vision of the future, and the courage to explain how you want to live your life.

Self-confidence and a good relationship with yourself must come first. Peace and a relaxed state are second; like your stove, you must be warmed up for a good relationship. Next, your expectation should be exact: It will work. It's a fact: The more you practice, the luckier you become. You will make decisions quickly, and they will be firm, no wobbling; you'll know what you're making and how to make it.

Example 2: Driving a car.

1. Know your car. In other words, know yourself. Personal development helps you notice your thoughts, habits, beliefs, and patterns of actions.
2. Know the rules of the road. To drive safely, you need to stay in the right lane and stop at the red lights. For good things to start to happen in your life, you need to be in the right place with the right people.
3. Know where your destination is. It's your job to know what you want. Which direction you need to go depends on it.

What subject needs to improve the most? What do you need to study? What example do you need to have? Who has done it?

Three Things to Remember

1. Start with what you have and focus on multiplying it. It's never a "zero"; it's a "one", even if it's not obvious to you at first. Look and you will find something to begin with. No matter how small or big it is, you need to find it. You always have a "one" to move into "two."
2. Build the foundation of what you want to create.
3. Know what the right order is.

CHAPTER 9

Discipline and Habits Should Serve You

There are lots of different kinds of discipline; they are the puzzles of one big picture of your future. Apply what you learned; it can be one of the disciplines. Next can be to start from one good habit and create a second and third, to improve your life constantly. You need to see the big picture. Adopt all kinds of disciplines. Practice the discipline to get up early and the discipline to do what you say you'll do. Practice to be motivated and see the good in everything. Practice to focus on what is essential now. Practice to succeed. Practice one discipline at a time.

Declare your inner power. Agree with yourself, and commit to your decision. Say you will do it, and don't think or talk about it endlessly. If for some reason you don't do it, come up with a fresh idea to create necessary change. Believe in yourself. Important: it's not a destination; it's the journey that matters.

Habits

Whatever you do over and over again will become part of your automatic behavior, which we call a habit. Your reaction to something good or something awful will likely be the same at different points in time in various situations because your body remembers how to behave in that scenario and goes on autopilot. You want to start to notice your automatic reaction and teach yourself to react differently. In the beginning, you have to work on it, but later, your body will do it automatically.

Believe it or not, you can have a habit of struggling or fighting, and life will never disappoint you in delivering all the conflicts you need to support this fire of emotions. You need to trust the significant power, known as God or the universe.

Did you know it's possible to habitually be upset, angry, hungry, or thirsty? By repetition of the same action and adding emotional impact, you create a habit; it became a part of your automatic program. For example, you are upset about something, and someone constantly reminds you of it. Now, this person becomes a trigger; as soon as you make contact with this individual, your emotions start running automatically. Control your thoughts first and then your feelings when you're angry or upset with somebody. When you notice it, be prepared to meet this person; plan what you will do to avoid the reaction you had before.

You need a starting point for commitment to live in a particular way. It can be tomorrow morning, or September 1, or the New Year; if it's today, you need to know the date. Create your unique ritual of preparation for the dedication. You can take a bath with rose petals or put on a new dress or get a new haircut. Come up with an idea to remember the moment when things start to change in your favor.

Chapter 10
The Power of Focus

The law of accumulation says that every great achievement is an accumulation of many small accomplishments. You create the momentum from "one" to "two" and from "two" to "three." Continuously look for what you want to see and what you want to feel. Focus on things that will make your dream come alive and make you feel closer to your ideal life today than you were yesterday. In the beginning, you may see just a small hint of something that nobody notices but you; then, there will be two hints, and then three, and so on.

Exercise to keep your focus:

To grow your success and put yourself in the right mindset, try this counting-up mantra: "From 1 to 2; from 2 to 3; from 3 to 4; from 4 to 5; from 5 to 6; from 6 to 7; from 7 to 8; from 8 to 9." Also, intentionally look for support of your victories and blessings; #1 and #2 and #3 and so on.

When focusing on fixing your problems, try this: "From 9 to 8; from 8 to 7; from 7 to 6; from 6 to 5; from 5 to 4; from 4 to 3; from 3 to 2; from 2 to 1; and from 1 to none."

To help keep focused and take control, you need a measuring instrument, like journaling your achievements, big and small wins, and task deadlines. Focus on counting how many good things happen to you in a week, in a month. You think there is nothing; think again. Remember that it's all around you; you need to focus to see it.

An excellent example of focus:

Layers of a city: Imagine a paper pad. Every sheet of paper

represents one layer of the city, and the pad represents the city itself. In this city, one sheet of paper will be power lines; the other will be pipelines; others will be streets, trees, traffic, dust, and flowers. All of them piled up make a city. There are layers of lawyers, teachers, criminals, adults, kids, and animals.

If you don't see all of the city but only part of it, you'll see a teachers association or a layer of schools. An electrician will know power lines better than everyone else. His focus will be on power lines. A plumber will know pipes and fittings. A detective will focus on details of crimes. These won't be noticeable to other people but are very important to them.

It's the magic of focusing on things. If there's a young mom, she will know more about kindergartens and playgrounds than anyone else. It looks like everyone lives in their own world. Pay attention and learn about your ideal vision for life and find the layer of it in the real world.

Give yourself a direct order to look for the particular details of love, joy, money, a specific partner, and outstanding success.

Another example is hidden images in a three-dimensional picture.

I will give you a task: find me thirty-eight images of a crocodile in the picture. Will you look until you catch all thirty-eight of them? If I had said look for some crocodiles, chances are you would stop at ten or twenty. You would say that there are no more, that not a single one left behind.

It's important to explain what you want clearly. An example

of the *wrong* way to explain yourself would be: Your husband gives you the grocery list. You get to the store and look at the list; it says: "Don't buy mustard. We already have it."

Distractions and Focus

Distractions knock you off course, so you need to focus on one thing at a time until the task is complete. It is possible to get caught up in distractions and forget even your deepest desires. You need to return to your compass all the time. The wind blows hard, and you get off the road, or you start talking and get distracted and forget what you wanted to build.

Remove all distractions. Surround yourself with reminders: pictures, notes, affirmations, alarms, and anything that helps you remember. Focus on one essential thing. It's impossible to focus on two or more.

Imagine a laser that's divided into two streams. The power of the laser is divided by two. Now imagine a stream of water in the shower. The power of the water stream will be different in different settings. Focus on one thing at a time. It must be your most important priority at this moment. Energy flows where attention goes.

For example, I want to have a family, but I don't want a man to dominate over me. In my experience, men are stronger, bigger, and more powerful. My friend had an experience of being disrespected by her boyfriend. It means your subconscious mind will avoid any possibility for you to have a family.

In this case, I would suggest giving a task to yourself to find an example of a good relationship and a joyful family. When you start to notice people who have it, and notice how they behave, you'll start to prepare yourself for having a good family.

There are thoughts in your mind that are old; they are not true for your life today. It's possible they are not even yours. You heard them many times, and they stuck with you to the point where you adopted them as yours. There is a difference between being three years old, fifteen years old, and your age today. You can realize you kept old thoughts and beliefs that are not true anymore and do not serve you. Learn to adopt new thoughts.

What is holding you back?

Your answer _____

Three Things to Remember

1. The more precise your focus, the more powerful it is.
2. Get help; everything you know and everybody you know can help you. Every thought and every action should focus on completing your task.
3. Know what the end reslut needs to look like, what you need to do for it, and when it must happen. Urgency creates pressure, and that is power.

CHAPTER 11

Rhythm and Regularity

Ask yourself, if I do this regularly, what will happen in one week/one month/one year/ten years?

Sometimes, we think, It's so easy to do that, I won't even bother, or It's so difficult to do that; I can't even imagine myself doing it. Maybe it's the small details that create quality for our lives.

- Think good about yourself.
- Observe everything: how you feel, what you think and say, even how you breathe. Yes, breathe; you heard me right.
- Take a run in the morning to make sure you are in a good mood.
- Learn to be in control of your thoughts and emotions. Learn how to switch your emotions, interrupt the flow of negative thoughts, be in alignment, and have peace.
- Be educated on the topics of health, relationships, and money management.
- Imagine the future to the point it becomes your reality.
- Doing something new all the time; it's a part of the growing process.
- Pay attention to the person you spend most of your time with. What do you learn from this person? Do you feel good about yourself and this person? How often does this happen?

- Listen to smart people all the time. It does not matter whether you finished school a long time ago and have a university degree.
- Read books, take courses, upgrade your knowledge regularly.
- Keep yourself busy, and you'll have no time to become older.
- Look for a way for things you play in to become your work. There are no small details when you look at your life.
- Write down your goals; read them daily; speak them loudly; look at them during the day many times; imagine they come true.
- Adjust your behavior and prepare for failures. Set up your mind to be in the right place at the right time and have the information you need when you need it.
- Think, *I couldn't do it before, but now I'm learning how. I thought it was impossible, but now I have the feeling that I can do anything.*
- Use the right vocabulary: have a positive mind-set, use effective management, see the vision of your future, improve, achieve, expand your comfort zone, work on yourself.

All of this will help you to do more things, and work not harder but smarter. Successful people look for excellent quality, believe they deserve the best, and never accept things they don't need in their life; they let it go fast.

You need to believe in yourself and trust you can enhance places and people around you; everything you touch will become gold. You sell yourself your dream. Feel it, remember it, and visualize the result in one month, in three months, in a year, and in two years.

Work smart. There is a time for planning, and there is a time for implementing. Write things down, look at them daily, and do them in order. Don't look for a way to stop working; look for a way to turn your hobby into your work.

Act as a successful person, and you will become one faster than you ever thought possible. The gap between them and you must be closed. We are the same; we are human. We all have families and friends, and we all have to deal with ourselves.

Pay attention to the patterns of your behavior. If this is your pattern of behavior: "Eat. Sleep. Shop. Watch TV. Repeat," change it to: "Relax. Plan. Expect good things to happen. Act. Repeat." With this pattern, you feel good about yourself, and you become awesome.

If you only do things from time to time, it won't give you the result you want. A good routine creates a pattern of automatic and low inertia; it will double your power, and you'll save some of your energy.

Do you eat regularly? It's easier if you know what time you

are eating every day. The more you eat, the more you want to eat; the more you complain about something, the more you want to complain; the more you practice success, the more you want to succeed.

Your Instruments

- ✓ Awareness. Journal your days to learn your thoughts, feelings, habits, and reactions.
- ✓ Recognition. You have the power to change your thoughts, your breathing rhythm, your reactions, and your actions. There is God; there is something more powerful than we are. You need to do your part to take care of your "garden", choose what to plant, and let God make the plants and trees grow. God takes care of it regularly.
- ✓ Reminders. Remove all distractions. Surround yourself with reminders: pictures, notes, affirmations, like-minded people, and so on. Exercise to control your thoughts and your feelings with somebody else or yourself. One by one, take things under control; it's become part of your new life.
- ✓ Inner Power. Claim your inner power instead of your intellect. Calm your mind with meditations, affirmations, walks, drawing, stitching, playing with kids, or doing something nice for yourself. Your inner

self knows how to do it, and everything is possible for you. Smart people are real people, just like you. They're a little bit ahead.
- ✓ Imagination. Exercise your imagination every day like you exercise your muscles. Read your plan every morning and evening. Do brainstorming exercises. Do exercises to boost your creativity.

How Magic Happens for Things to be Done Easily and Nicely

- ✓ Get inspiration. What do you want?
- ✓ Become energized. Special feelings attached to this wish.
- ✓ Get clarity. The vision of your future.
- ✓ Be ready. Preparation process, practicing success.
- ✓ Expect good things in your life. Remove resistance.

It's a matter of what happens before you create an experience you have now or in the future. Be ready to be ready. Be all set to enjoy life, and you will. Be prepared, in case Plan A fails, to pull out Plan B. Focus on the bigger picture; don't create a big deal from a small stumble or misconception.

People will see it as a miracle: Suddenly your dream house appears, or you are famous overnight, or your account is full of money. People around you will wonder what happened to you.

They believe it happened overnight; everything that occurs before is not exposed step by step to them; it is not visible.

When your soul, mind, and body agree to create a better life and a better you. When your thoughts, feelings, beliefs, and actions are on the same page, you become happy and successful. There is no "Yes," "No," "Maybe," or "I don't know." You know it's "Yes." You are going to do it. You feel right about your idea, and you act. If at this moment, you think you are far from perfect, but you are sincere about your knowledge, your direction in life, and you work on yourself, people will like you and want to help you.

You need to work on improving and empowering yourself; this alone will remove resistance in you, which keeps you from taking actions. Your confidence will support you all the time. If you are not confident at this moment, start to build your confidence. It's easy: start to compliment yourself on three things you did well today; later, find four, and then five. Your self-confidence will grow very fast and have solid ground.

Ask yourself, who can help me today?

Your answer _____

How can I make it easier?

Your answer _____

How can I do what I need to do faster?

Your answer _____

Practice it; make it a part of your daily life. You will work out your muscle of creativity; you will expend your ideas generator. You will learn so much about yourself, and your life will become easier.

Chapter 12

Declare Ownership of Your Life

One by one, take control over your thoughts, feelings, actions, and patterns of behavior.

Your Body: Thoughts, feelings, actions, and patterns of behavior. By repeating them, they become habits. Habits run on autopilot, unless you want to change programming and create a new habit.

Your Emotions: Thoughts, feelings, actions, and patterns. By repeating them, they become habits. Later on, they turn on automatically when contacted by a trigger.

Your Health: Thoughts, feelings, actions, and patterns of behavior. Repetition of it becomes a style of life.

Your Energy: Thoughts, feelings, actions, and patterns of behavior. By repeating them, it becomes a habit to express yourself in a certain way.

Your Finances: Thoughts, feelings, actions, and patterns of behavior. Repetition of it becomes a habit to have or not have money.

For example, I will give you a house; it's yours! Will you inspect it? Will you take care of it and make it suitable and comfortable for you? Will you make it more valuable or will you destroy it? It's the same with your life. It's yours; you are the owner. Therefore, if someone is abusing it, it's your responsibility to protect it. If it's you that isn't protecting or supporting yourself, you need to stop it. Reevaluate, restore, renew, and create a better life; become happier.

When you care for yourself, everyone around starts to care for you. What needs to happen for you to have value in your life? Life is not your conditions; even if you were deprived, you're still alive. Even if somebody mistreated, disrespected, or abused you, you are still alive. You have the power to change terms, protect your life, and care for it. Expect good things for yourself; start from imagining it is possible.

Relationship Mastery

Relationship with Yourself

Create a good relationship with yourself. It is the most important relationship in your life.

Am I good enough? Do I feel like I am worthy to have the best? How can I build respect for myself?

Every so often, you need to upgrade and transform your thoughts, emotions, and overall life. What needs to be done for you to feel you are amazing?

Relationships with Others

You touch anything, and it becomes gold; remember that. Any person who connects with you can become a better person because of you. You see them as remarkable people; you expect them to be excellent; you enjoy spending time with them. If you help people feel good about themselves, they will like you and care for you. It's easy to be judgmental or doubt others and yourself, but you know where it's leading.

Your relationship with people around you is an important part of your life. You may want to find a new job or a partner. Ask yourself, What I will learn from those people? What kind of people do they associate with? Do I want to become part of it?

You can make everyone you meet better and make them feel better about themselves and the world overall. It's the same in reverse; those people can make you better. Remember the order: First a good relationship with yourself, positive self-talk; second, positive expectations; third, good intentions.

Emotional Mastery

I was thinking about what we know about happiness. We all want to be happy and healthy, and yet when we look around, we see all types of people: happy and grim, healthy and unhealthy; full of energy and exhausted people without any power in them. Why is that? Some people don't pay attention to small things. They don't take time to notice what makes them happy or unhappy.

Emotional intelligence is about learning how to control your emotions.

To get you to a peaceful state, you need to want it; you need to search for peace. You need to recognize stress and avoid it when you can.

How well you rest the night before will affect how you react today to everything. Many times, you do this without even realizing this stress can be released. A million minor things can go wrong, and then you have a huge problem. You cannot explain a week later why you start to cry after a button fell off your jacket.

Manage how you see the situation, mindfully imagining things happening at a different time in a different place or with different people; sometimes, it looks stupid or funny. It will show you the situation from a different perspective.

Do you make your body stronger, healthier, and more restful to better handle situations? What do you do to relax? Ask yourself is it necessary to be like that? Is this the best I can be? Fix the problem so it doesn't need to be fixed again. Use your senses to help you; therefore, ask yourself, how does it feel? Is it pure and light energy? Is it flow?

Find support for yourself: there is some higher power than you. Find a friend or family member who supports you, take a class, or find some other way; everything will help you become stronger and happier. Increase your standards. Create a new image of yourself.

Money Mastery

Example: Dancing with a partner.

Imagine you want to have a good time and maybe find a new friend. You go to a club or a party and dance with someone attractive. What happens first? You after say hello and introduce yourself, after you dance if you are interested in this person, you try to stay in touch later.

Apply these details for creating a relationship with money; notice that you were in a particular mood, feeling good about yourself and a potential partner. You went somewhere to meet other people. Next, you show interest. Your relationship with money can be the same. You go to a place where you can make the amount of money you want. You feel good about yourself and the money overall, show a healthy interest in money, and keep in touch, gradually building a relationship with money.

Recall these actions:

- ✓ You had the intention to get together with someone. You get it straight: you feel good about yourself and the partner, you feel good about you and your partner being together.
- ✓ You keep in touch all the time, not like once a year.

- ✓ You prepare: cheer up, dress up, and smile because you want to be loved.
- ✓ Every interaction feels good. Having a partner who connects with you is a good feeling.

These are synonyms of a relationship: communication, connection, and attitude.

Definition: Attitude is a settled way of thinking or feeling about someone or something, typically one that is reflecting in a person's behavior.

Just like a romantic relationship, keep in touch with money and build a relationship with it. Do not let it disappear on the day after payday or show no interest in it or act as if you don't care whether you have money or not. Your attitude towards money must be that it's not the most important thing in your life, but it is valuable, and you need it.

With some time, you can build something with money, which will make the relationship stronger.

Money management has the same system as anything. Start with your vision of what would make you happy. Take over control, organize the flow, and adjust your actions.

Time Mastery

How much time do you need? Know where it goes. Know that your time is valuable; be wise with how you spend it.

How much time does it cost for you to be distracted? Every time you're distracted for an hour, you need twenty minutes to return to the previous state. Where do you spend your time? Is it a hobby, entertainment, education, business, fighting, having fun?

I once spoke with my daughter and said, "I don't learn anything new from seminars or audiobooks; they just make me feel good," and she replied, "Treat it as entertainment, not to spend hours of your time when you need to work on your business project or call your customers."

Epilogue

Six Strings of a Guitar, as Strings of Your Life

You and your life, like an artist and guitar, create a unique melody and reveal your highest finesse as a master.

What is the process for the guitar to reveal a melody?

- ✓ It needs you as a player.
- ✓ You must be in the right state; the song must be relevant to you.
- ✓ You need to like to play this melody.

- ✓ Keep in touch with the instrument and audience; stay at it long enough.
- ✓ You need to have emotional connections with everyone around you.

Strings of your life to create amazing sound:

1. Initiative and right mind-set
2. Preparation and practice
3. Vibration
4. Feeling good
5. Simply playing
6. Connection with audience

The first string is initiative/mind-set.

First, you have the impulse; you want to play. You try here and there, and you learn what you need to do to play it well. Next, choose at what level you want to play the instrument. Do you want to play for fun or professionally? Realize that it's all about you; without you, the guitar will not play. You need to be there every time; you need to show up for the instrument to sound. Every time, you need to be in the state of *I am*, not *I was* or *I will be when…* I am now.

For example, imagine a string of pearls. The thread that holds together this necklace is a most important thing. You are the thread that holds together the necklace of events and experiences of life.

The second string is preparation.

All the strings of the guitar must be tuned. If one of them is too tight or too loose, the instrument will not perform properly. In real life, it's health, relationship, money, and self-expression. You are not touching all of the strings you're working on; adjust only the one necessary. If you can't control your emotions, the area you must improve on is emotional intelligence; if your money is not under your control, work on developing this area.

The third string is vibration.

You can't play the song if the vibration of the strings is wrong; you touch them to stop the unwanted vibration and start again with a particular rhythm.

Applying this lesson to your life, when you notice something wrong, you need to stop accepting things that are not getting you to where you want to be. You must get tired of being tired and decided to do something about it; you must be fed up with the struggle. You're sick of being sick, and suddenly, all your concentration is focused on getting better. You get tired of being broke and miserable, and you work your way out.

It's not easy to decide this emotionally because you realize it's a friend you love, frustrating you consistently, and as much as you enjoy spending time with them, you hate when they do certain things. It may be delicious sweets that you love, but they are not serving your vision for your body. And again, you don't even enjoy the dessert when you're eating it because you know it's the same old story: after you eat, you will regret it.

The fourth string is feeling good.

You need to like the melody you're trying to play, so it has a special connection with your feelings. You must enjoy the music and want to play. In life, you need to know what you love to do, what you want to experience, and what makes you happy. Connect to the cause. The driving force must be because it makes you happy, so you'll do it.

The fifth string is to simply play.

Keep in touch with the guitar. When you stop, the melody goes away. Any relationship will die if you lose connection; some of them take longer than others, but the feelings will fade away with time.

The better the musician, the better the melody. Even after you train yourself up to a very high level, you need to practice all the time. When you don't keep in touch with guitar for performing, you lose the skills to play it.

The sixth string is the connection with the audience.

The audience creates a good performer.

Your melody helps you and helps others to enjoy life, to tune into the good vibrations of your feelings. You need to realize you are a part of something huge: part of our planet, part of our society, part of your generation, and part of your family history.

One more thing: we never work on a guitar; we play it.

CPSIA information can be obtained
at www.ICGtesting.com
Printed in the USA
LVHW050000120419
613887LV00014B/89